THIS CRUISE JOURNAL BELONGS TO:

PRE-CRUISE PLANNING

TIPS TO SAVE MONEY ON YOUR NEXT CRUISE

1. **Plan your trip for off-peak seasons, if possible.** You'll usually find the most affordable dates when the kids are in school and outside of holidays. Not only will you save some money, but you'll likely travel on less crowded ships. Also, plan your trip far in advance (or very last minute). Some people plan their cruises YEARS in advance, simply because rates are based on availability and demand.

2. **Buy Travel Insurance.** Don't be afraid of the upfront cost of travel insurance. Forgoing it can cause you more money in the long run. Your health insurance may not cover you when you hit international waters or you may need to cancel your trip for unexpected reasons. Travel insurance can protect you in cases such as these. Use your travel agent to find the best and most affordable policy. Using a travel credit card that has travel insurance is great option as well.

3. **Prepay gratuities, but make sure not to tip too much while on your cruise.** Educate yourself if you've already paid for your gratuities. It's nice to give the bartender an extra dollar or two for great service, but read to see if their tip is already covered with the prepaid package. For example, some drink packages have tips included. If you're not careful, you could end up tipping twice. Do tip when you check in bags and for room service delivery.

4. **Prepay as much as you can up front.** Paying for excursions, food and drink packages in advance will save you more money than if you paid for them while you board. Check your cruise ship's vacation planner/account and check for specials and deals. In addition, it will help you to budget for these expenses and spread them out over a schedule that works for you.

5. **Look for cruise port parking alternatives.** When you consider that parking at the cruise port could cost you an average of $15-20 a day, it may be best to compare prices elsewhere. Look at parking at a park and cruise hotel. If you live nearby, have someone to drop you off. Also, consider Uber or Lyft to drop you off and pick you up.

6. **Compare booking excursions with the ship and outside providers.** Yes, ships offer assurance that they won't leave you if you're at an excursion and running late, however so do other reputable companies. Compare prices with excursions from the ship as well as those off-site as well. You could save plenty by doing so.

7. **Fly in a day before embarkment day and fly out a day after.** Delays happen and a late flight could cause you to miss your cruise or cause you to lose money to change your flight. Give yourself some time (and a piece of mind) by flying in a day before and leaving the day after you return. The hotel cost will be minimal compared to having to pay cancellation fees or for transportation to the next port.

8. **Put your phone in airplane mode.** Forgetting to do this could cost you a lot of money while on board. Your cell phone will try to roam to find a connection. The cellular fees will cause you a lot of stress if you forget.

9. **Book entertainment and spa visits on port days.** You may find substantial savings onboard on port days. Not only will the ship be less crowded while everyone is out at port, the crew may offer deals for those who stay on board. Plan to stay on the ship during ports you're not interested in visiting.

10. **Check shipboard account regularly for charges/mistakes.** Don't wait until the last day to check your account, if you do, you'll be in a long line on the last day. Don't do it.

CRUISE SAVINGS

WE'RE SAVING FOR:

AMOUNT NEEDED:

OUR GOAL DATE:

DEPOSIT TRACKER

AMOUNT DEPOSITED: **DATE DEPOSITED:**

$

$

$

$

$

$

$

$

$

$

CRUISE SAVINGS

DEPOSIT TRACKER

AMOUNT DEPOSITED: **DATE DEPOSITED:**

$

$

$

$

$

$

$

$

$

$

$

$

$

$

CRUISE SAVINGS

DEPOSIT TRACKER

AMOUNT DEPOSITED: **DATE DEPOSITED:**

$

$

$

$

$

$

$

$

$

$

$

$

$

$

CRUISE DETAILS

NOTES

TO DO:

CRUISE DETAILS & REMINDERS:

CRUISE DETAILS

NOTES

TO DO:

CRUISE DETAILS & REMINDERS:

CRUISE DETAILS

NOTES

TO DO:

CRUISE DETAILS & REMINDERS:

ALL ABOARD!

PRE-CRUISE TO DO LIST & CHECKLIST

1 MONTH BEFORE

2 WEEKS BEFORE

1 WEEK BEFORE

2 DAYS BEFORE

24 HOURS BEFORE

DAY OF TRAVEL

CRUISE COUNTDOWN

MONTH: _____   YEAR: _____

M	T	W	T	F	S	S

CRUISE COUNTDOWN

MONTH: _____   YEAR: _____

M	T	W	T	F	S	S

CRUISE COUNTDOWN

MONTH: YEAR:

M	T	W	T	F	S	S

CRUISE COUNTDOWN

MONTH: _____   YEAR: _____

M	T	W	T	F	S	S

CRUISE COUNTDOWN

MONTH: _____   YEAR: _____

M	T	W	T	F	S	S

CRUISE COUNTDOWN

MONTH: _____   YEAR: _____

M	T	W	T	F	S	S

CRUISE COUNTDOWN

MONTH: _____   YEAR: _____

M	T	W	T	F	S	S

CRUISE COUNTDOWN

MONTH: YEAR:

M	T	W	T	F	S	S

CRUISE COUNTDOWN

MONTH: _____   YEAR: _____

M	T	W	T	F	S	S

CRUISE COUNTDOWN

MONTH: YEAR:

M	T	W	T	F	S	S

CRUISE COUNTDOWN

MONTH: _____   YEAR: _____

M	T	W	T	F	S	S

CRUISE COUNTDOWN

MONTH: _____   YEAR: _____

M	T	W	T	F	S	S

FLIGHT INFORMATION

DATE:	DESTINATION:

AIRLINE:	
BOOKING NUMBER:	
DEPARTURE DATE:	
BOARDING TIME:	
GATE NUMBER:	
SEAT NUMBER:	
ARRIVAL / LANDING TIME:	

DATE:	DESTINATION:

AIRLINE:	
BOOKING NUMBER:	
DEPARTURE DATE:	
BOARDING TIME:	
GATE NUMBER:	
SEAT NUMBER:	
ARRIVAL / LANDING TIME:	

CRUISE PACKING CHECKLIST

CLOTHING	✓	ESSENTIALS	✓

CRUISE PACKING CHECKLIST

CLOTHING FOR HER	✓	CLOTHING FOR HIM	✓

ESSENTIALS	✓	FOR THE JOURNEY	✓
		IMPORTANT DOCUMENTS	✓

CRUISE PACKING CHECKLIST

CLOTHING FOR HER	✓	CLOTHING FOR HIM	✓
T-Shirts &, Tank Tops & Blouses		T-Shirts & Tank Tops	
Sundresses		Shorts	
Flip Flops, Sandals & Heels		Swim Wear	
Shorts & Pants		Jeans, Khakis	
Swimsuit & Cover Up		Formal Attire (dress shirt, shoes, etc.)	
T-Shirts &, Tank Tops & Blouses		Belt	
Aqua/Swimming Shoes		Tie	
Bras, Panties & Socks		Sandals / Sneakers	
Sunhat		Visor, Baseball Cap	
Sunglasses		T-Shirts &, Tank Tops & Blouses	
Formal Attire		Sunglasses	
Jewelry		Socks & Underwear	
ESSENTIALS	✓	**FOR THE JOURNEY**	✓
Lanyard		Carry On Bag	
Suntan Lotion		Cash / Local Currency	
Medication (motion sickness, etc.)		Credit Cards	
Travel Mug / Water Bottle		Phone Charger	
		Backpack	
		IMPORTANT DOCUMENTS	✓
		Passport & ID	
		Cruise Documents & Boarding Pass	
		Flight Information	

CRUISE PACKING CHECKLIST

CLOTHING	✓	ESSENTIALS	✓

CRUISE PACKING CHECKLIST

CLOTHING FOR HER	✓	CLOTHING FOR HIM	✓

ESSENTIALS	✓	FOR THE JOURNEY	✓
		IMPORTANT DOCUMENTS	✓

CRUISE PACKING CHECKLIST

CLOTHING FOR HER	✓	CLOTHING FOR HIM	✓
T-Shirts &, Tank Tops & Blouses		T-Shirts & Tank Tops	
Sundresses		Shorts	
Flip Flops, Sandals & Heels		Swim Wear	
Shorts & Pants		Jeans, Khakis	
Swimsuit & Cover Up		Formal Attire (dress shirt, shoes, etc.)	
T-Shirts &, Tank Tops & Blouses		Belt	
Aqua/Swimming Shoes		Tie	
Bras, Panties & Socks		Sandals / Sneakers	
Sunhat		Visor, Baseball Cap	
Sunglasses		T-Shirts &, Tank Tops & Blouses	
Formal Attire		Sunglasses	
Jewelry		Socks & Underwear	
ESSENTIALS	✓	**FOR THE JOURNEY**	✓
Lanyard		Carry On Bag	
Suntan Lotion		Cash / Local Currency	
Medication (motion sickness, etc.)		Credit Cards	
Travel Mug / Water Bottle		Phone Charger	
		Backpack	
		IMPORTANT DOCUMENTS	✓
		Passport & ID	
		Cruise Documents & Boarding Pass	
		Flight Information	

CRUISE EXCURSION PLANNER

ACTIVITY / EXCURSION OVERVIEW:

EST COST OF EXCURSION:

INCLUSIONS:	✓	**EXCLUSIONS:**	✓
FOOD & DRINK:	☐		☐
TRANSPORTATION:	☐		☐
GRATUITY:	☐		☐

ACTUAL COST:

IMPORTANT INFORMATION:

CONTACT: PHONE #:

MEET UP TIME: WHAT TO BRING:

ADDRESS:

CRUISE EXCURSION PLANNER

ACTIVITY / EXCURSION OVERVIEW:

EST COST OF EXCURSION:

INCLUSIONS:	✓	**EXCLUSIONS:**	✓
FOOD & DRINK:	☐		☐
TRANSPORTATION:	☐		☐
GRATUITY:	☐		☐

ACTUAL COST:

IMPORTANT INFORMATION:

CONTACT: PHONE #:

MEET UP TIME: WHAT TO BRING:

ADDRESS:

CRUISE EXCURSION PLANNER

ACTIVITY / EXCURSION OVERVIEW:

EST COST OF EXCURSION:

INCLUSIONS:	✓	**EXCLUSIONS:**	✓
FOOD & DRINK:	☐		☐
TRANSPORTATION:	☐		☐
GRATUITY:	☐		☐

ACTUAL COST:

IMPORTANT INFORMATION:

CONTACT: PHONE #:

MEET UP TIME: WHAT TO BRING:

ADDRESS:

CRUISE EXCURSION PLANNER

ACTIVITY / EXCURSION OVERVIEW:

EST COST OF EXCURSION:

INCLUSIONS:	✓	**EXCLUSIONS:**	✓
FOOD & DRINK:	☐		☐
TRANSPORTATION:	☐		☐
GRATUITY:	☐		☐

ACTUAL COST:

IMPORTANT INFORMATION:

CONTACT: PHONE #:

MEET UP TIME: WHAT TO BRING:

ADDRESS:

CRUISE EXCURSION PLANNER

ACTIVITY / EXCURSION OVERVIEW:

EST COST OF EXCURSION:

INCLUSIONS:	✓	**EXCLUSIONS:**	✓
FOOD & DRINK:	☐		☐
TRANSPORTATION:	☐		☐
GRATUITY:	☐		☐

ACTUAL COST:

IMPORTANT INFORMATION:

CONTACT: PHONE #:

MEET UP TIME: WHAT TO BRING:

ADDRESS:

CRUISE EXCURSION PLANNER

ACTIVITY / EXCURSION OVERVIEW:

EST COST OF EXCURSION:

INCLUSIONS:	✓	**EXCLUSIONS:**	✓
FOOD & DRINK:	☐		☐
TRANSPORTATION:	☐		☐
GRATUITY:	☐		☐

ACTUAL COST:

IMPORTANT INFORMATION:

CONTACT: _____ PHONE #: _____

MEET UP TIME: _____ WHAT TO BRING: _____

ADDRESS: _____

CRUISE EXCURSION PLANNER

ACTIVITY / EXCURSION OVERVIEW:

EST COST OF EXCURSION:

INCLUSIONS:	✓	**EXCLUSIONS:**	✓
FOOD & DRINK:	☐		☐
TRANSPORTATION:	☐		☐
GRATUITY:	☐		☐

ACTUAL COST:

IMPORTANT INFORMATION:

CONTACT: PHONE #:

MEET UP TIME: WHAT TO BRING:

ADDRESS:

CRUISE PORT PLANNER

DESTINATION: DATE:

THINGS TO DO / SEE:

☐
☐
☐
☐
☐
☐
☐

WHERE TO EAT:

☐
☐
☐
☐
☐
☐
☐

TRANSPORTATION DETAILS:

☐
☐
☐
☐
☐

OTHER INFORMATION:

☐
☐
☐
☐
☐

RETURN TO SHIP BY:

CRUISE PORT PLANNER

DESTINATION: DATE:

THINGS TO DO / SEE:

☐
☐
☐
☐
☐
☐
☐

WHERE TO EAT:

☐
☐
☐
☐
☐
☐
☐

TRANSPORTATION DETAILS:

☐
☐
☐
☐
☐

OTHER INFORMATION:

☐
☐
☐
☐
☐

RETURN TO SHIP BY:

CRUISE PORT PLANNER

DESTINATION: DATE:

THINGS TO DO / SEE:

☐
☐
☐
☐
☐
☐
☐

WHERE TO EAT:

☐
☐
☐
☐
☐
☐
☐

TRANSPORTATION DETAILS:

☐
☐
☐
☐
☐

OTHER INFORMATION:

☐
☐
☐
☐
☐

RETURN TO SHIP BY:

CRUISE PORT PLANNER

DESTINATION: DATE:

THINGS TO DO / SEE:

☐
☐
☐
☐
☐
☐
☐

WHERE TO EAT:

☐
☐
☐
☐
☐
☐
☐

TRANSPORTATION DETAILS:

☐
☐
☐
☐
☐

OTHER INFORMATION:

☐
☐
☐
☐
☐

RETURN TO SHIP BY:

CRUISE PORT PLANNER

DESTINATION: DATE:

THINGS TO DO / SEE:

☐
☐
☐
☐
☐
☐
☐

WHERE TO EAT:

☐
☐
☐
☐
☐
☐
☐

TRANSPORTATION DETAILS:

☐
☐
☐
☐
☐

OTHER INFORMATION:

☐
☐
☐
☐
☐

RETURN TO SHIP BY:

CRUISE
FUN

CRUISE PLANNER

WEEK OF:

MONDAY	TUESDAY	WEDNESDAY	THURSDAY

TO DO	TO DO	TO DO	TO DO

MEALS	MEALS	MEALS	MEALS

FRIDAY	SATURDAY	SUNDAY	NOTES

TO DO	TO DO	TO DO	

MEALS	MEALS	MEALS	MEALS

CRUISE PLANNER

WEEK OF:

MONDAY	TUESDAY	WEDNESDAY	THURSDAY
TO DO	TO DO	TO DO	TO DO
MEALS	MEALS	MEALS	MEALS

FRIDAY	SATURDAY	SUNDAY	NOTES
TO DO	TO DO	TO DO	
MEALS	MEALS	MEALS	MEALS

CRUISING TO DO LIST

CRUISING TO DO LIST

CRUISING TO DO LIST

CRUISE BUCKET LIST

PLACES I WANT TO VISIT:

THINGS I WANT TO SEE:

TOP 3 DESTINATIONS:

CRUISE BUCKET LIST

PLACES I WANT TO VISIT:

THINGS I WANT TO SEE:

TOP 3 DESTINATIONS:

CRUISE ITINERARY

Monday

Tuesday

Wednesday

Thursday

Friday

Saturday

Sunday

CRUISE ITINERARY

Monday

Tuesday

Wednesday

Thursday

Friday

Saturday

Sunday

CRUISE OVERVIEW

MONTH:

MONDAY	TUESDAY	WEDNESDAY	THURSDAY	FRIDAY	SATURDAY	SUNDAY

CRUISE ACTIVITIES

WEEKLY ACTIVITY TRACKER:

	M	T	W	T	F	S	S
	◯	◯	◯	◯	◯	◯	◯
	◯	◯	◯	◯	◯	◯	◯
	◯	◯	◯	◯	◯	◯	◯
	◯	◯	◯	◯	◯	◯	◯
	◯	◯	◯	◯	◯	◯	◯
	◯	◯	◯	◯	◯	◯	◯
	◯	◯	◯	◯	◯	◯	◯
	◯	◯	◯	◯	◯	◯	◯
	◯	◯	◯	◯	◯	◯	◯
	◯	◯	◯	◯	◯	◯	◯
	◯	◯	◯	◯	◯	◯	◯
	◯	◯	◯	◯	◯	◯	◯
	◯	◯	◯	◯	◯	◯	◯
	◯	◯	◯	◯	◯	◯	◯

CRUISE ACTIVITIES

WEEKLY ACTIVITY TRACKER:

	M	T	W	T	F	S	S
	○	○	○	○	○	○	○
	○	○	○	○	○	○	○
	○	○	○	○	○	○	○
	○	○	○	○	○	○	○
	○	○	○	○	○	○	○
	○	○	○	○	○	○	○
	○	○	○	○	○	○	○
	○	○	○	○	○	○	○
	○	○	○	○	○	○	○
	○	○	○	○	○	○	○
	○	○	○	○	○	○	○
	○	○	○	○	○	○	○
	○	○	○	○	○	○	○
	○	○	○	○	○	○	○

CRUISE ACTIVITIES

WEEKLY ACTIVITY TRACKER:

	M	T	W	T	F	S	S
	◯	◯	◯	◯	◯	◯	◯
	◯	◯	◯	◯	◯	◯	◯
	◯	◯	◯	◯	◯	◯	◯
	◯	◯	◯	◯	◯	◯	◯
	◯	◯	◯	◯	◯	◯	◯
	◯	◯	◯	◯	◯	◯	◯
	◯	◯	◯	◯	◯	◯	◯
	◯	◯	◯	◯	◯	◯	◯
	◯	◯	◯	◯	◯	◯	◯
	◯	◯	◯	◯	◯	◯	◯
	◯	◯	◯	◯	◯	◯	◯
	◯	◯	◯	◯	◯	◯	◯
	◯	◯	◯	◯	◯	◯	◯
	◯	◯	◯	◯	◯	◯	◯

DAILY ACTIVITY PLANNER

DAILY ITINERARY

ACTIVITY: _____

TIME: _____

LOCATION: _____

WEATHER: ☀ ⛅ 🌦 ☁ ⛈

MEAL PLANNER

DAILY EXPENSES

TOTAL COST: [_____]

TOP ACTIVITIES

TIME:	SCHEDULE:

NOTES:

DAILY ACTIVITY PLANNER

DAILY ITINERARY

ACTIVITY: _____

TIME: _____

LOCATION: _____

WEATHER: ☀ ⛅ 🌦 ☁ ⛈

MEAL PLANNER

DAILY EXPENSES

_____ _____

_____ _____

_____ _____

_____ _____

_____ _____

TOTAL COST: [_____]

TOP ACTIVITIES

TIME:	SCHEDULE:

NOTES:

DAILY ACTIVITY PLANNER

DAILY ITINERARY

ACTIVITY: _____

TIME: _____

LOCATION: _____

WEATHER: ☀ ⛅ 🌦 ☁ ⛈

MEAL PLANNER

TOP ACTIVITIES

TIME:	SCHEDULE:

DAILY EXPENSES

TOTAL COST: [   ]

NOTES:

DAILY ACTIVITY PLANNER

DAILY ITINERARY

ACTIVITY: _____

TIME: _____

LOCATION: _____

WEATHER: ☀ ⛅ 🌧 ☁ ⛈

MEAL PLANNER

DAILY EXPENSES

_____ _____

_____ _____

_____ _____

_____ _____

_____ _____

TOTAL COST: [_____]

TOP ACTIVITIES

TIME:	SCHEDULE:

NOTES:

DAILY ACTIVITY PLANNER

DAILY ITINERARY

ACTIVITY: _____

TIME: _____

LOCATION: _____

WEATHER: ☀ ⛅ 🌦 ☁ ⛈

MEAL PLANNER

DAILY EXPENSES

TOTAL COST: [   ]

TOP ACTIVITIES

TIME:	SCHEDULE:

NOTES:

DAILY ACTIVITY PLANNER

DAILY ITINERARY

ACTIVITY: _____

TIME: _____

LOCATION: _____

WEATHER: ☀ ⛅ 🌦 ☁ ⛈

MEAL PLANNER

DAILY EXPENSES

_____ _____

_____ _____

_____ _____

_____ _____

_____ _____

TOTAL COST: [   ]

TOP ACTIVITIES

TIME:	SCHEDULE:

NOTES:

DAILY ACTIVITY PLANNER

DAILY ITINERARY

ACTIVITY: _____

TIME: _____

LOCATION: _____

WEATHER: ☀ ⛅ 🌦 ☁ ⛈

MEAL PLANNER

TOP ACTIVITIES

TIME:	SCHEDULE:

DAILY EXPENSES

TOTAL COST: [   ]

NOTES:

DAILY ACTIVITY PLANNER

DAILY ITINERARY

ACTIVITY: _____

TIME: _____

LOCATION: _____

WEATHER:

MEAL PLANNER

DAILY EXPENSES

TOTAL COST:

TOP ACTIVITIES

TIME:	SCHEDULE:

NOTES:

DAILY ACTIVITY PLANNER

DAILY ITINERARY

ACTIVITY: _____

TIME: _____

LOCATION: _____

WEATHER: ☀ ⛅ 🌦 ☁ ⛈

MEAL PLANNER

TOP ACTIVITIES

TIME: SCHEDULE:

DAILY EXPENSES

TOTAL COST: [   ]

NOTES:

DAILY ACTIVITY PLANNER

DAILY ITINERARY

ACTIVITY: _____

TIME: _____

LOCATION: _____

WEATHER: ☀ ⛅ 🌦 ☁ ⛈

MEAL PLANNER

DAILY EXPENSES

_____   _____

_____   _____

_____   _____

_____   _____

_____   _____

TOTAL COST: [   ]

TOP ACTIVITIES

TIME:	SCHEDULE:

NOTES:

DAILY ACTIVITY PLANNER

DAILY ITINERARY

ACTIVITY: _____

TIME: _____

LOCATION: _____

WEATHER: ☀ ⛅ 🌦 ☁ ⛈

MEAL PLANNER

TOP ACTIVITIES

TIME:	SCHEDULE:

DAILY EXPENSES

_____ _____

_____ _____

_____ _____

_____ _____

TOTAL COST: [_____]

NOTES:

DAILY ACTIVITY PLANNER

DAILY ITINERARY

ACTIVITY: _____

TIME: _____

LOCATION: _____

WEATHER: ☀ ⛅ 🌦 ☁ ⛈

MEAL PLANNER

DAILY EXPENSES

_____   _____

_____   _____

_____   _____

_____   _____

TOTAL COST: [   ]

TOP ACTIVITIES

TIME:	SCHEDULE:

NOTES:

DAILY ACTIVITY PLANNER

DAILY ITINERARY

ACTIVITY: _____

TIME: _____

LOCATION: _____

WEATHER: ☀ ⛅ 🌦 ☁ ⛈

MEAL PLANNER

DAILY EXPENSES

TOTAL COST: [   ]

TOP ACTIVITIES

TIME:	SCHEDULE:

NOTES:

DAILY ACTIVITY PLANNER

DAILY ITINERARY

ACTIVITY: _____

TIME: _____

LOCATION: _____

WEATHER: ☀️ ⛅ 🌦️ ☁️ ⛈️

MEAL PLANNER

TOP ACTIVITIES

TIME:	SCHEDULE:

DAILY EXPENSES

_____ _____

_____ _____

_____ _____

_____ _____

TOTAL COST: [   ]

NOTES:

MY CRUISE AGENDA

MY CRUISE AGENDA

MY CRUISE AGENDA

MY CRUISE AGENDA

MY CRUISE AGENDA

MY CRUISE AGENDA

MY CRUISE AGENDA

MY CRUISE AGENDA

NEW FRIENDS

CRUISE FRIENDS

FRIENDS ARE FOREVER

NAME:

PHONE NUMBER:

ADDRESS:

CABIN #:

FRIENDS ARE FOREVER

NAME:

PHONE NUMBER:

ADDRESS:

CABIN #:

FRIENDS ARE FOREVER

NAME:

PHONE NUMBER:

ADDRESS:

CABIN #:

FRIENDS ARE FOREVER

NAME:

PHONE NUMBER:

ADDRESS:

CABIN #:

There's Nothing Like Cruising Life!

CRUISE FRIENDS

FRIENDS ARE FOREVER

NAME:

PHONE NUMBER:

ADDRESS:

CABIN #:

FRIENDS ARE FOREVER

NAME:

PHONE NUMBER:

ADDRESS:

CABIN #:

FRIENDS ARE FOREVER

NAME:

PHONE NUMBER:

ADDRESS:

CABIN #:

FRIENDS ARE FOREVER

NAME:

PHONE NUMBER:

ADDRESS:

CABIN #:

There's Nothing Like Cruising Life!

CRUISE FRIENDS

FRIENDS ARE FOREVER

NAME:

PHONE NUMBER:

ADDRESS:

CABIN #:

FRIENDS ARE FOREVER

NAME:

PHONE NUMBER:

ADDRESS:

CABIN #:

FRIENDS ARE FOREVER

NAME:

PHONE NUMBER:

ADDRESS:

CABIN #:

FRIENDS ARE FOREVER

NAME:

PHONE NUMBER:

ADDRESS:

CABIN #:

There's Nothing Like Cruising Life!

CRUISE FRIENDS

FRIENDS ARE FOREVER

NAME:

PHONE NUMBER:

ADDRESS:

CABIN #:

FRIENDS ARE FOREVER

NAME:

PHONE NUMBER:

ADDRESS:

CABIN #:

FRIENDS ARE FOREVER

NAME:

PHONE NUMBER:

ADDRESS:

CABIN #:

FRIENDS ARE FOREVER

NAME:

PHONE NUMBER:

ADDRESS:

CABIN #:

There's Nothing Like Cruising Life!

CRUISE FRIENDS

FRIENDS ARE FOREVER

NAME:

PHONE NUMBER:

ADDRESS:

CABIN #:

FRIENDS ARE FOREVER

NAME:

PHONE NUMBER:

ADDRESS:

CABIN #:

FRIENDS ARE FOREVER

NAME:

PHONE NUMBER:

ADDRESS:

CABIN #:

FRIENDS ARE FOREVER

NAME:

PHONE NUMBER:

ADDRESS:

CABIN #:

There's Nothing Like Cruising Life!

CRUISE FRIENDS

NAME:

PHONE NUMBER:

ADDRESS:

CABIN #:

NAME:

PHONE NUMBER:

ADDRESS:

CABIN #:

NAME:

PHONE NUMBER:

ADDRESS:

CABIN #:

NAME:

PHONE NUMBER:

ADDRESS:

CABIN #:

There's Nothing Like Cruising Life!

CRUISE
JOURNAL
PAGES

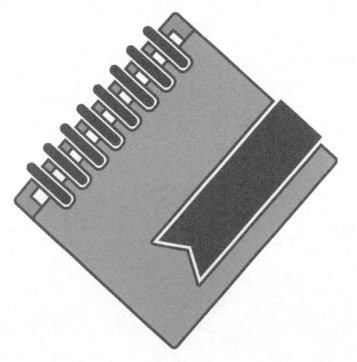

MY CRUISE JOURNAL

DATE:

What I Did Today:

Highlight of the Day:

Thoughts & Reflections:

MY CRUISE JOURNAL

DATE:

What I Did Today:

Highlight of the Day:

Thoughts & Reflections:

_____

_____

_____

_____

_____

_____

_____

_____

_____

_____

_____

_____

_____

MY CRUISE JOURNAL

DATE:

What I Did Today:

Highlight of the Day:

Thoughts & Reflections:

MY CRUISE JOURNAL

DATE:

What I Did Today:

Highlight of the Day:

Thoughts & Reflections:

_____

_____

_____

_____

_____

_____

_____

_____

_____

_____

_____

_____

MY CRUISE JOURNAL

DATE:

What I Did Today:

Highlight of the Day:

Thoughts & Reflections:

MY CRUISE JOURNAL

DATE:

What I Did Today:

Highlight of the Day:

Thoughts & Reflections:

MY CRUISE JOURNAL

DATE:

What I Did Today:

Highlight of the Day:

Thoughts & Reflections:

MY CRUISE JOURNAL

DATE:

What I Did Today:

Highlight of the Day:

Thoughts & Reflections:

_____

_____

_____

_____

_____

_____

_____

_____

_____

_____

_____

_____

_____

_____

_____

MY CRUISE JOURNAL

DATE:

What I Did Today:

Highlight of the Day:

Thoughts & Reflections:

MY CRUISE JOURNAL

DATE:

What I Did Today:

Highlight of the Day:

Thoughts & Reflections:

MY CRUISE JOURNAL

DATE:

What I Did Today:

Highlight of the Day:

Thoughts & Reflections:

MY CRUISE JOURNAL

DATE:

What I Did Today:

Highlight of the Day:

Thoughts & Reflections:

MY CRUISE JOURNAL

DATE:

What I Did Today:

Highlight of the Day:

Thoughts & Reflections:

MY CRUISE JOURNAL

DATE:

What I Did Today:

Highlight of the Day:

Thoughts & Reflections:

MY CRUISE JOURNAL

DATE:

What I Did Today:

Highlight of the Day:

Thoughts & Reflections:

_____

_____

_____

_____

_____

_____

_____

_____

_____

_____

_____

_____

_____

MY CRUISE JOURNAL

DATE:

What I Did Today:

Highlight of the Day:

Thoughts & Reflections:

_____

_____

_____

_____

_____

_____

_____

_____

_____

_____

_____

_____

_____

MY CRUISE JOURNAL

DATE:

What I Did Today:

Highlight of the Day:

Thoughts & Reflections:

MY CRUISE JOURNAL

DATE:

What I Did Today:

Highlight of the Day:

Thoughts & Reflections:

MY CRUISE JOURNAL

DATE:

What I Did Today:

Highlight of the Day:

Thoughts & Reflections:

MY CRUISE JOURNAL

DATE:

What I Did Today:

Highlight of the Day:

Thoughts & Reflections:

MY CRUISE JOURNAL

DATE:

What I Did Today:

Highlight of the Day:

Thoughts & Reflections:

MY CRUISE JOURNAL

DATE:

What I Did Today:

Highlight of the Day:

Thoughts & Reflections:

_____

_____

_____

_____

_____

_____

_____

_____

_____

_____

_____

_____

_____

_____

Made in the USA
Columbia, SC
17 September 2023

22986726R00072